Mason Jar Recipes: 60 Super #Delish Mason Jar Recipes & Seasoning Mixes

RHONDA BELLE

DEDICATION

To Foodies Everywhere...Enjoy & Be Well!

Table of Contents

ACKNOWLEDGEMENTS

To the love of my life, Johnny, thank you for the joy you bring to each day.
You are Mommy's greatest inspiration.

JAR RECIPE TIPS

Mason jar meals are fun to create and also make great gifts! Most of these recipes require wide mouth, 1-quart Mason jars with attached flip lids that offer an extra tight seal. Others may specify the use of jars that have a lid and ring assembly, particularly if you are actually baking a dish within the jar itself. Read all instructions in full before beginning any recipe.

For final presentation, tie brightly colored ribbon, decorative raffia, wooden spoons, and instruction tags around the mouth of your sealed jar. For a country craft look, consider cutting rings of bright cloth, with a few cotton balls tucked underneath, and secure the cloth around the mouth of the jar with a pretty ribbon. This creates a "poufy" appearance and beautifully crafty design.

Here's a tip...alternate the layers of ingredients so that the distinctive colors shine through the jars. This makes a pretty display. Contents can shift, so pack them in tightly using a spoon or mallet to keep your design intact. For example, after measuring brown sugar in a recipe, crumble it between your fingers for uniform texture. Pack it into the jar firmly to prevent the remaining baking mix from sifting downward and destroying your design.

When using lids and rings, keep lids in piping hot water until they're used for sterilization purposes. This will help preserve contents properly for a longer shelf life.

Sealed jars may be stored with other canned food or placed in a freezer. If you are concerned about the safety of storing your fully cooked jar cakes, an alternative is to store them in the freezer. The cake is safe to eat as long as the jar remains vacuum-sealed. Unsealed jars should be stored in the refrigerator and eaten within 2 weeks. Enjoy!

COOKIES & CAKES

Apple Cookie Mix
2 ¼ cups all-purpose flour
1 cup brown sugar
¾ teaspoon ground cinnamon
¾ cup raisins
¾ cup chopped nuts
½ teaspoon salt
½ teaspoon baking soda

Combine flour, salt, cinnamon and baking soda - stir well. Place flour mixture in a clean mason jar. Pack down tight using a spoon so everything will fit in the jar. Add other ingredients, one item at a time, packing each layer down. Seal tightly. Decorate as desired.

Tag Instructions: Whip ¾ cup of butter or shortening until light and fluffy. Add 1 egg and ½ cup applesauce and beat until mixed. Stir in jar contents until well combined. Drop teaspoon of dough on a greased cookie sheet. Bake for 8 - 12 minutes at 350 degrees. Remove and enjoy!

Candy Oatmeal Bars Mix
1 cup biscuit & baking mix
½ cup packed light brown sugar (see cook's note)
½ cup packed dark brown sugar
½ cup old-fashioned oats
½ cup mini M&M's candies

In 1-quart wide-mouth glass jar, gently layer and pack ingredients in the order listed, starting with oats. If there is any space left after adding the last ingredient, add more candies to fill the jar. Seal tightly and decorate as desired. *Yield 16 bars.*

Tag Instructions: To prepare, empty contents of jar into medium bowl. Stir in 1 stick melted butter, 1 large egg and 1 teaspoon vanilla. Press into baking pan coated with cooking spray. Bake at 350 degrees for 18 to 22 minutes or until bars are light golden brown and center is almost set. Remove and allow to cool at room temperature. Enjoy!

Carrot Cake Mix

3 cups all-purpose flour
2 teaspoon powdered vanilla
2 teaspoon baking soda
2 cups sugar
1 tablespoon cinnamon
½ cup chopped pecans
¼ teaspoon nutmeg

Combine and blend ingredients in a small bowl. Store in an airtight container. Decorate as desired. *Yield: 1 13x9-inch cake.*

Tag Instructions: To prepare carrot cake, you will also need:

3 large eggs
3 cups grated carrots
1 ½ cups vegetable oil
1 (8-ounce) can crushed pineapple

Preheat oven to 350 degrees and grease 13x9-inch pan. Place jar contents in large mixing bowl. Make a well in the center of the mix & add the oil, eggs, carrots & pineapple. Blend until smooth. Pour into the prepared pan & bake for 40 to 50 minutes, or until a toothpick inserted into center comes out clean. Remove from oven, cool and enjoy!

Choco-Candy Cookies

2 cups flour
1 teaspoon powdered vanilla
1 teaspoon baking soda
½ cup sugar
½ cup brown sugar, firmly packed

Combine all ingredients in a medium bowl. Whisk the ingredients together until they are evenly distributed, making sure all brown sugar lumps are crushed. Store in an airtight container. Decorate if desired. *Yield: Enough for 3 dozen cookies.*

Tag Instructions: To make cookies, add the following to the mix:

1 cup unsalted butter or margarine, softened
1 large egg
1 cup candy bar chunks (Reese's peanut butter cups, Butterfinger bars, or other candy of your choice)

Preheat oven to 350 degrees. In the large bowl of an electric mixer, beat the butter until it is smooth. Add the egg, and continue beating until the egg is combined. Add the Candy Cookie Mix and candy bar chunks and blend on low just until the cookie mix is incorporated. Form the cookies into 1 ½-inch balls & place them 2 inches apart on an ungreased cookie sheet. Bake for 10 to 12 minutes, until golden on the edges. Remove from oven, and cool on cookie sheet for 2 minutes. Enjoy!

Chocolate-Chip-Lover Cookies

½ cup chopped pecans
½ cup chocolate chips
½ cup white chocolate chips
1/3 cup brown sugar packed
3/8 cup white sugar
½ teaspoon soda
¼ teaspoon salt
1/6 cup cocoa
1 ¼ cups all-purpose flour

Place in this order in a 1-quart jar. Pack tightly and ensure an airtight seal. You can decorate the jar with your own special tags, bright colored ribbons, etc.

Tag Instructions: To make cookies, you will also need:

1 tablespoon milk
1 stick melted butter
1 egg
½ teaspoon vanilla

Combine all ingredients with jar contents. Place 1-inch balls on cookie sheet and press flat using a fork. Cook at 350 degrees for 8 minutes. Remove from oven, cool completely and enjoy!

Chocolaty Peanut Butter Cookie Mix

1½ cups packed confectioners' sugar
1½ cups all-purpose flour
1 teaspoon baking powder
1 cup packed brown sugar
¾ cup cocoa
¼ teaspoon salt

In a separate bowl, mix together the flour, baking powder and salt. Layer ingredients in order given in a wide mouth 1-quart canning jar. Clean the inside of the jar with a dry paper towel after adding the confectioners' sugar and after adding the cocoa powder. Be sure to pack everything down firmly before adding the flour mixture for a tight fit. Seal and decorate jar if desired. *Yield: 3 dozen cookies.*

Tag Instructions: To prepare cookies, empty desired amount of cookie mix into large mixing bowl. Use your hands to thoroughly blend mix. Add: ½-cup butter (not margarine) softened at room temperature. Add ½-cup creamy peanut butter, 1 egg, slightly beaten, and 1 teaspoon of vanilla. Mix until completely blended. You will need to use your hands to finish mixing. Shape into walnut sized balls and place 2 inches apart on a parchment lined baking sheets. Press balls down with a fork. Bake at 350 degrees for 9 to 11 minutes until edges are browned. Cool and enjoy!

Cinnamon Pancake Mix

4½ teaspoon ground cinnamon
3 tablespoon sugar
3 cups all-purpose flour
2 tablespoon baking powder
1¼ teaspoon salt
In a 1 quart jar, combine all ingredients and seal jar, adding dried fruits if desired to help fill small gaps. Seal tightly and decorate if desired.

Tag Instructions: To prepare pancakes, combine ¾ cup milk, 1 egg, and 2 tablespoons salad oil in medium bowl. With fork, blend in 1 1/3 cups pancake mix until moistened, but still lumpy. Cook on lightly greased griddle or skillet. Enjoy! *Yield: About ten 5" pancakes.*

Citrus Candy Cookie Mix

¾ cup sugar
½ cup packed brown sugar
1¾ cups flour mixed with 1 teaspoon baking powder and ½ teaspoon baking soda
1½ cups orange slice candies, quartered (wrap in plastic wrap)
Layer ingredients in jar in the order specified. Press each layer firmly in place using a spoon before adding next ingredient. Seal tightly and decorate with ribbon, raffia, etc. as desired.

Tag Instructions: To make cookies, first remove candies from jar and set aside. Empty cookie mix in large mixing bowl; stir to combine. Add ½ cup softened butter, 1 egg slightly beaten and 1teaspoon vanilla; mix until completely blended. Stir in orange candies last. Roll dough into walnut-sized balls. Place 2 inches apart on a lightly greased cookie sheet. Bake at 375 degrees for 12 to 14 minutes or until edges are lightly browned. Cool 5 minutes on baking sheet. Remove to wire racks to cool completely. Enjoy! *Yield: 2-½ dozen cookies.*

Coffee Mug Cake

1 cake mix any flavor

1 (4 serving size) instant pudding mix (not sugar free) - *Try lemon, vanilla, chocolate, coconut or butterscotch flavor options*

Place dry cake mix and dry pudding mix into a large bowl and blend well with a whisk. This will be about 4 - 4 ½ cups dry mix and will make 8-9 coffee cup cake mixes. Place ½ cup dry mix into a sandwich bag shifting mix into a corner of the bag and tie it there with a twist tie. Continue making packets until all your dry mix is used.

Tag instructions: To prepare mug cake, select a large, microwave safe coffee cup that can hold 1½ cups of water. Generously spray inside of coffee cup with cooking spray. Empty contents of large packet into cup. Add 1 egg white, 1 tablespoon oil, and 1 tablespoon water to dry mix. Mix 15 seconds, carefully mixing in all the dry mix. Microwave on full power 2 minutes.

To prepare cake glaze, you will need:

French Vanilla Coffee Mate

1/3 cup powdered sugar

1 ½ teaspoon dry flavoring (such as powdered lemonade mix, powdered orange breakfast drink mix, cocoa powder)

While cake is cooking, place glaze ingredients into a very small container and add 1 ½ teaspoon water. Mix well. When cake is done, pour glaze over cake in cup. Enjoy while warm.

Cornflake Cookie Mix

2 ½ cups coconut

1 ½ cups corn flake cereal

1 ¼ cups white sugar

¼ teaspoon salt

Place sugar and salt in a clean mason jar. Pack down tight tightly using a spoon. Add other ingredients, one item at a time, packing each layer down. *Cornflakes should be added last* so that they are not crushed. Put the lid on the jar and decorate as desired.

Tag Instructions: To prepare cookies, whip 3 egg whites until stiff. Add ½ teaspoon of vanilla extract. Stir in the jar contents until well combined. Drop teaspoon of dough on an ungreased cookie sheet. Bake for 15 minutes at 325 degrees. Remove from oven and let cool. Enjoy!

Cranberry Smilies

½ cup plus 2 tablespoon flour

½ cup rolled oats

½ cup flour mixed with ½ teaspoon baking soda and ½ teaspoon salt

1/3 cup plus 1 tablespoon packed brown sugar

1/3 cup white sugar
½ cup dried cranberries
½ cup pecans
Layer the ingredients in a 1-quart jar in order as listed. Seal tightly.
Tag Instructions: To prepare, cream together: ½-cup butter (softened), 1 egg, and 1-tsp. vanilla. Add the entire jar of ingredients and mix together by hand until well blended. Drop batter in heaping spoonfuls onto the greased baking sheet. Bake at 350 degrees for 8-10 min. Enjoy!

Fantasy Cookie Mix

1 ¾ cups all-purpose flour
1 ½ cups vanilla baking chips
¾ cup white sugar
½ teaspoon baking soda
½ teaspoon baking powder
½ cup orange-flavored drink mix (such as Tang)
Combine the flour with the baking soda and baking powder. Starting with the Tang, then sugar, vanilla chips and ending with the flour mixture. Layer the ingredients (alternate color for best presentation) in a clean glass wide mouth quart sized jar. Press each layer firmly in place before adding the next ingredient. Seal tightly and decorate jar if desired. *Yield 2 ½ dozen cookies.*
Tag Instructions: Preheat oven to 375 degrees. Empty contents into a large mixing bowl. Add ½ cup softened butter, 1 egg slightly beaten and teaspoon vanilla extract. Mix until completely blended. Roll heaping tablespoonfuls into balls. Place 2 inches apart on a lightly greased baking sheet. Bake at 375 degrees for 12 to 14 minutes or until tops are very lightly browned. Cool for 5 minutes on the sheet then remove cookies to wire racks to cool completely. Enjoy!

Honolulu Cookie Mix

1/3 cup sugar
½ cup packed brown sugar
1/3 cup packed flaked coconut
2/3 cup chopped macadamia nuts
2/3 cup chopped dates
2 cups flour mixed with 1 teaspoon baking soda and 1 teaspoon baking powder
Layer ingredients in jar in order given. Press each layer firmly in place before adding next ingredient. Seal tightly and decorate jar if desired.
Tag Instructions: To make cookies, place jar contents into a large mixing bowl; stir to combine. Add ½ cup softened butter, 1 egg slightly beaten and 1 teaspoon vanilla; mix until completely blended. Roll dough into walnut-sized balls. Place 2 inches apart on a lightly greased cookie sheet. Press cookie down slightly with the heel of your hand. Bake at 350° for 11 to 13 minutes or until

edges are lightly browned. Cool 5 minutes on baking sheet. Remove to wire racks to cool completely. Enjoy! *Yield: 2-½ dozen cookies.*

Oatmeal Raisin Cookie Mix
1 teaspoon baking powder
1 cup flour
1 ¼ cup raisins
1 ¼ cup oats
½ cup sugar
½ cup packed brown sugar
¼ teaspoon salt

Combine flour, salt and baking soda - stir well. Place flour mixture in a clean mason jar. Pack tightly using a spoon or a mallet. Add other ingredients, one item at a time, packing each layer down. Put the lid on the jar, sealing tightly, and decorate with ribbon, raffia, your tags, etc. as desired.

Tag Instructions: To prepare cookies, whip ½ cup of butter until light and fluffy. Add 1 egg and 1 teaspoon vanilla and beat until mixed. Stir in the ingredients from this jar until well combined. Drop 1 tablespoon of dough on a greased cookie sheet. Bake for 15 minutes at 350 degrees. Remove, cool, serve and enjoy!

Old-Fashioned Oatmeal Cookie Mix
2 cups rolled oats
1 teaspoon ground cinnamon
1 teaspoon baking soda
1 cup all-purpose flour
¾ cup packed brown sugar
¾ cup butterscotch baking chips
½ teaspoon salt
½ teaspoon ground nutmeg
½ cup white sugar

In large bowl, combine flour, cinnamon, nutmeg, baking soda and salt. Layer ingredients in order given in canning jars, layering flour mixture last. Seal tightly. Decorate as desired.

Tag Instructions: To make cookies, empty mix into large mixing bowl, mix thoroughly. Add 3/4-cup butter, softened, 1 beaten egg, and 1 teaspoon vanilla. Mix until completely blended. Form 1-inch balls and place 2 inches apart on ungreased cookie sheet. Bake at 350 degrees until edges are lightly browned, about 10-12 minutes. Cool 5 minutes on cookie sheet, then transfer to wire rack to cool completely. Enjoy! *Yield: Makes3 dozen cookies.*

Peanuty Goodness Cookie Mix

8 large Reese's peanut butter cups candies cut into ½ inch pieces (wrap in plastic wrap)

1 ¾ cups flour mixed with 1 teaspoon baking powder and ½ teaspoon baking soda

¾ cup sugar

¼ cup packed brown sugar

Layer ingredients in jar in order given. Press each layer firmly in place using a spoon before adding next ingredient. Seal tightly and decorate your jar, if desired.

Tag Instructions: To prepare cookies, remove candies from jar and set aside. Empty jar contents in large mixing bowl; stir to combine. Add ½ cup softened butter, 1 egg slightly beaten and 1-tsp. vanilla; mix until completely blended. Stir in candies. Roll dough into walnut-sized balls. Place 2 inches apart on a lightly greased cookie sheet. Bake at 375 degrees for 12 to 14 minute or until edges are lightly browned. Cool 5 minutes on baking sheet. Remove to wire racks to cool completely. Enjoy! *Yield: 2-½ dozen cookies.*

Raisinette Cookie Mix

1¾ cups flour

1 teaspoon baking powder

1 cup chocolate covered raisins

¾ cup white sugar

½ teaspoon baking soda

½ cup packed brown sugar

½ cup milk chocolate chips

Mix together the flour, baking powder and baking soda. Layer ingredients in order given in a quart size wide mouth-canning jar. Press each layer firmly using a spoon to pack tightly. Seal tightly and decorate jar as desired. *Yield: 2½ dozen*

Tag Instructions: To prepare cookies, empty jar contents into large mixing bowl. Use hands to thoroughly blend. Add ½-cup butter (not margarine), softened at room temperature. Add 1 egg, slightly beaten and 1 teaspoon of vanilla. Mix until completely blended. Shape into walnut sized balls. Place 2 inches apart on a parchment lined cookie sheet. Bake at 375 degrees 13 to 15 minutes until tops are very lightly browned. Cool 5 minutes on baking sheet. Enjoy! *Yield: 2½ dozen cookies.*

Ranchero Cookies

1 teaspoon baking soda
1 teaspoon baking powder
1 cup semisweet chocolate chips
1 1/3 cups quick cooking oats
1 1/3 cups all-purpose flour
½ cup white sugar
½ cup packed brown sugar
½ cup chopped pecans
¼ teaspoon salt

Layer the ingredients in a 1-quart jar in the order given. Press each layer firmly with a spoon before adding the next one. Store in an airtight container. Decorate if desired.

Tag Instructions: To prepare cookies, preheat oven to 350 degrees. Grease cookie sheets. In a medium bowl, cream together ½ cup of butter, 1 egg, and 1 teaspoon of vanilla. Stir in the entire contents of the jar. Shape into walnut sized balls. Place 2 inches apart on the prepared cookie sheets. Bake for 11 to 13 minutes in the preheated oven. Remove, cool and enjoy!

Saturday Brownies

2/3 teaspoon salt
1⅛ cups flour, divided
1/3 cups cocoa powder
2/3 cups brown sugar
2/3 cups sugar
½ cup chocolate chips
½ cup white chocolate chips
½ cup walnuts or pecans

Wash, rinse and dry canning jars. Layer ingredients, packing tightly. Seal and decorate jar if desired.

Tag Instructions: To prepare brownies, preheat oven to 350 degrees. Grease one 9x9 baking pan. Pour the contents of the jar into a large bowl and mix well. Stir in 1 teaspoon vanilla, 2/3 cup vegetable oil and 3 eggs. Beat until just combined. Pour the batter into the prepared pan and bake at 350 degrees for 20 to 25 minutes. Remove, let cool and enjoy!

Sugar Cookie Extraordinaire

3¼ cups all-purpose flour
1¼ cups white sugar
¼ cup colored decorating sugar
2½ teaspoon baking powder
½ teaspoon salt

Combine flour, salt and baking powder - stir well. Place flour mixture in a clean mason jar. Pack tightly. Stir sugar and colored sugar together, add to the jar. Put the lid on the jar and decorate as desired.

Tag Instructions: Whip 2/3 cup of butter or shortening until light and fluffy. Add 2 eggs, 2 tablespoon milk and 1 teaspoon vanilla and beat until mixed. Stir in the ingredients from this jar until well combined. Roll into small balls and place on a greased cookie sheet. Flatten each ball slightly with a fork. Bake for 8 minutes at 350 degrees. Remove let cool and enjoy.

Trail Mix Cookie Mix

1/3 cup quick cooking oats
1/3 cup packed flaked coconut
1 teaspoon baking powder
1 cup raisins
¾ cup wheat germ
½ cup white sugar
½ cup packed brown sugar
½ cup all-purpose flour

Layer ingredients in order given in a 1-quart canning jar. Mix the flour and baking powder. Press each layer firmly in place for a tight fit. Seal tightly and decorate container with ribbon, etc. as desired.

Tag Instructions: To prepare cookies, empty jar of cookie mix into large mixing bowl. Use your hands to thoroughly blend mix. Add: ½-cup butter (not margarine) softened at room temperature. Mix in 1 egg, slightly beaten and 1 teaspoon vanilla. Mix until completely blended. Shape into walnut sized balls and place 2 inches apart on a sprayed cookie sheet. Bake at 350 degrees for 12 to 14 minutes until edges are lightly browned. Cool 5 minutes on baking sheet. Remove cookies and finish cooling. Enjoy! *Yield: 2 ½ dozen cookies.*

White Chocolate Macadamia Nut Cookie Mix

2 cups all-purpose flour
1¼ cups white sugar
1 cup white chocolate baking chips
½ teaspoon baking soda
½ teaspoon baking powder
½ cup chopped macadamia nuts

Mix flour, baking soda, baking powder. Layer ingredients in quart-size canning jars, flour mixture last. Seal tightly and decorate jar.

Tag Instructions: Empty cookie mix into mixing bowl. Add: ½ cup butter, softened, 1 beaten egg, and 1 teaspoon of vanilla. Mix until completely blended. Shape into 1-inch balls and place 2 inches apart on greased cookie sheets. Bake at 375 degrees for 12 to 14 minutes until tops are very lightly browned. Cool 5 minutes on baking sheet. Remove from oven to finish cooling. Enjoy!

CAKES-IN-A-JAR

Cake Parade in a Jar
2 cups flour
2/3 cup cocoa powder
¾ teaspoon salt
1 ½ teaspoon baking powder
1 1/3 cups sugar
In a large bowl, combine flour, salt, cocoa powder & baking powder. Layer ingredients in order listed in a 1-quart, wide mouth canning jar. Use a spoon to pack tightly. Seal jar tightly and decorate if desired.
Tag Instructions: T prepare cake, you will also need:
2 teaspoon vinegar
2 cups water
1 teaspoon vanilla
¾ cup vegetable oil
Stir cake ingredients together using a wire whisk or fork, making certain that all ingredients are completely mixed together. Bake at 350 degrees for 35 minutes. Frost as desired or serve sprinkled with powdered sugar, with fresh fruit on the side. #Delish!

Caramel Cake Surprise in a Jar
2/3 cup sugar
2/3 cup milk
2 cups brown sugar
2 sticks butter, softened
4 eggs
1 tablespoon vanilla
3 ½ cups flour
1 teaspoon baking powder
2 teaspoon baking soda
1 teaspoon salt
1 cup chopped nuts
To make jar cakes: In large bowl, cream sugars and butter with an electric mixer. Add eggs and mix well. Add milk and vanilla; stir well. Place dry ingredients and spices in a separate large bowl and blend with a whisk. Add creamed ingredients to dry ingredients and mix with whisk and spoon. Gently stir in nuts. Place 1 cup batter each into 6 well-greased, 1-pint wide-mouth canning jars. Wipe batter from rim. Place jars on a baking sheet. Bake at 325 degrees for 50 minutes, or until a toothpick inserted in center comes out clean.

Wipe rims to ensure they are clean for a proper seal. Place hot sterilized lids and rings on hot jars. Keep in refrigerator for prolonged storage. Enjoy!

Carrot Raisin Bread in a Jar

2 2/3 cups white sugar
2/3 cup vegetable shortening
2/3 cup water
4 eggs
2 cups shredded carrots
3 ½ cups all-purpose flour
¼ teaspoon cloves
1 teaspoon cinnamon
1 teaspoon baking powder
2 teaspoon baking soda
1 teaspoon salt
1 cup raisins

To make jar cakes: You will need six, wide-mouth pint-size canning jars with metal rings and lids. Sterilize jars, lids and rings according to manufacturer's directions. Grease inside of jar (not rim). Cream sugar and shortening, beat in eggs and water, add carrots. Sift together flour, cloves, cinnamon, baking powder, baking soda and salt; add to batter. Add raisins and mix. Pour exactly one cup of batter into each prepared jar. Place jars evenly spaced on a cookie sheet. Put into a pre-heated 325 degree oven for 45 minutes. While cakes are baking, bring a saucepan of water to a boil and carefully add jar lids. Remove pan from heat and keep hot until ready to use. Once baked, remove jars from oven one at a time keeping remaining jars in oven. Make sure jar rims are clean to ensure a proper seal. Place lids on jars and screw rings on tightly. Jars will seal as they cool. Cakes will slide right out when ready to serve. #Delish!

Chocolate Cake in a Jar

4 eggs
¾ cup unsweetened cocoa powder
3 cups white sugar
3 cups white flour
2 cups applesauce, unsweetened
1 teaspoon baking soda
1 tablespoon vanilla
1 stick plus 3 tablespoon butter or margarine
½ teaspoon baking powder
⅛ teaspoon salt

To make jar cakes: Pre-wash eight pint-sized, wide mouth canning jars according to manufacturer instruction. Grease insides of jar well. Beat together butter and half of sugar until fluffy. Add eggs and remaining sugar, vanilla and applesauce. Sift dry ingredients together and add to the applesauce mixture a little at a time: beat well after each addition. Pour one cup of batter into each jar and carefully remove any batter from the rims. Place jars in a preheated 325 degree oven and bake for 40 minutes. While cakes are baking, bring a saucepan of water to a boil and carefully add jar lids. Remove pan from heat and keep lids hot until ready to use. When the cakes have finished baking, remove jars from oven. Place hot lids on hot jars (be careful), and screw rings on tightly. Jars will seal as they cool. Cakes will slide right out when ready to serve. Enjoy!

Pina Colada Cake in a Jar
4 eggs, whipped
3 1/3 cups unbleached flour
3 ½ cups packed brown sugar
1 teaspoon baking soda
1 cup shredded coconut
1 cup margarine, softened
1 ½ teaspoon baking powder
1 (20 ounces) crushed can pineapple
½ cup rum

To make jar cakes: Preheat oven at 325. Before starting batter, <u>wash eight 1-pint wide mouth canning jars with lids</u> according to manufacturer's instructions. Generously prepare jars with cooking spray and flour. Drain pineapple for 10 minutes, reserving juice. Puree drained pineapple in a blender. Measure out 1 ½ cups puree, adding a little juice if necessary to make 1 ½ cups. Set puree aside. Discard remaining juice. In a mixing bowl, combine applesauce, half brown sugar until light and fluffy. Beat in eggs and pineapple puree. Set aside. In another mixing bowl, combine flour, baking powder, and baking soda. Gradually, add to pineapple mixture in thirds, beating well with each addition. Stir in coconut. Spoon 1 level cupful of batter into each jar. Carefully wipe rims clean to ensure a proper seal, then place jars on baking sheet. Bake 40 minutes. Keep lids in piping hot water until they're used. When done, remove jars from oven one at a time. Wipe rims with a moistened paper towel. Carefully put lids and rings in place, then screw tops until tightly shut. Place jars on a wire rack; they will seal as they cool. Decorate as desired. Cakes slide right out when ready to use. Enjoy!

Pumpkin Cake in a Jar
2/3 cup shortening
2 2/3 cups sugar
4 eggs
2 cups canned pumpkin
2/3 cup water

3 1/3 cups flour
½ teaspoon baking powder
1 ½ teaspoon salt
1 teaspoon ground cloves
½ teaspoon ground allspice
1 teaspoon ground cinnamon
2 teaspoon baking soda
1 cup chopped walnuts

To make jar cakes: Preheat oven to 325 degrees. Cream shortening and sugar together, adding sugar slowly. Beat in eggs, pumpkin, and water; set aside. In another bowl, stir together flour, baking powder, salt, cloves, allspice, cinnamon, and baking soda. Add to pumpkin mixture and stir well. Stir in nuts. Grease <u>8 pint size, wide mouth jars well and fill each jar about half full</u>. Place jars on baking sheet and bake for approximately 45 minutes. While baking, sterilize lids by placing in boiled water until ready to use. When done, remove jars from oven, and wipe the sealing edge of the jars. Place lids on jars and close tightly with the ring. Jars will seal as they cool. Decorate as you wish with ribbon, raffia, tags, etc. Cakes slide right out when ready to eat. Enjoy!

MEALS & SNACKS

Apples & Cinnamon Instant Oatmeal
Pinch of salt
6 teaspoons sugar
6 tablespoons chopped dried apples
6 plastic sandwich bags
3 cups quick oats
1 ¾ teaspoons cinnamon

Put ½-cup oats in blender and blend at high speed until powdery. Reserve in a small bowl, then process another ½-cup oats. Into each bag, put ¼ cup unchopped oats, 2 tablespoon powdered oats, and a scant ¼-tsp. salt. Seal and store packets in an airtight container. Decorate if desired.

Tag Instructions: To make oatmeal, empty a packet in bowl and add ¾ cups boiling water. Stir and let stand 2 minutes. Enjoy!

Buttermilk Pancake Mix
8 teaspoon baking powder
8 cups all-purpose flour
4 teaspoon baking soda
2 teaspoon salt
2 cups buttermilk powder
½ cup granulated sugar

Sift the ingredients together well. Store in a container with a tight-fitting lid. Decorate if desired. Use within 6 months. *Yield: 10 cups of mix.*

Tag Instructions: To make buttermilk pancakes, add:
1 egg, beaten
2 tablespoon vegetable oil
1-cup water, or more as needed.
1½ cups Buttermilk Pancake Mix

In a medium bowl, combine egg, oil, and 1-cup water. With a wire whisk, stir in Pancake Mix until blended. Let stand 5 minutes. Stir in additional water for a thinner batter. Lightly oil and preheat griddle. Pour about 1/3-cup batter onto hot griddle for each pancake. Cook until edge is dry and bubbles form. Turn with a wide spatula. Cook 35 to 45 seconds longer until browned on both sides. Repeat with remaining batter. *Yield: about 10 four-inch pancakes.*

Cinnamon Spice Instant Oatmeal
Pinch of salt
6 teaspoons sugar
6 plastic sandwich bags
3 cups quick oats
1 teaspoon nutmeg
1 ¾ teaspoons cinnamon

Put ½-cup oats in blender and blend at high speed until powdery. Reserve in a small bowl, then process another ½-cup oats. Into each bag, put ¼ cup unchopped oats, 2 tablespoon powdered oats, and a scant ¼-tsp. salt. Seal and store packets in an airtight container. Decorate if desired.

Tag Instructions: To make oatmeal, empty a packet in bowl and add ¾ cups boiling water. Stir and let stand 2 minutes. Enjoy!

Coconut Cream Pudding Mix
4 cups sugar
3 cups nonfat dry milk
3 cups cornstarch
1 teaspoon salt
1 teaspoon coconut extract
1 ½ cups shredded unsweetened coconut

Mix the extract and the shredded coconut in a small bowl until the extract is absorbed. Add the coconut to the other ingredients and store in airtight container. Decorate jar if desired.

Tag instructions: To prepare pudding, add 2/3-cup mix to 2 cups milk. Heat and stir constantly while boiling. Cool, then serve and enjoy!

Curried Rice Mix

2 tablespoon dried minced onion
1 cup long-grain rice
1 chicken bouillon cube, crumbled
½ teaspoon curry powder
¼ cup raisins

Layer the ingredients in the order given in a 1½-cup jar. Seal tightly, decorating jar if desired.

Tag Instructions: To make curried rice, add jar contents to 2 ½ cups water. In a medium saucepan bring the water to a boil. Add the rice mix. Cover and reduce the heat to a simmer for 20 minutes. Remove from heat. Serve warm. Enjoy!

Granola Groove

3 cups reg. rolled oats
1 cup shredded coconut
1 cup of any mixture of: shelled sunflower seeds, sesame seeds, or chopped pecans, filberts, peanuts, or cashews
¾ cup regular wheat germ
¾ cup chopped or sliced almonds
2/3 cup brown sugar, firmly packed
½ cup instant nonfat dry milk
1½ cups of any one or mix of: chopped dates, raisins, currants, chopped dried apricots, or chopped dried peaches

Layer dry ingredients into Mason jar and seal tightly. Decorate if desired.

Tag Instructions: To prepare granola, you will also need:

1/3 cup honey
¼ cup vegetable oil
Shortening to grease baking sheet

Preheat oven to 325 degrees. Grease a large baking pan or cookie sheet with solid shortening and set aside. Combine the first 7 ingredients in a bowl, mixing well. In a small saucepan, combine honey and oil; heat gently to dissolve honey. Pour honey mixture into the dry ingredients, stirring well to thoroughly coat and mix. Spread the mixture evenly over the baking pan and bake for 15-20 minutes. While baking, stir with a spatula (from outside in towards center) every 5 minutes. As granola cools, add the chopped dried fruit.

Cool well and enjoy. Store excess at room temperature air tight container. Enjoy!

Meat & Potatoes Dump Dinner

3 cups dehydrated potatoes
1/3 cup nonfat dry milk
1 teaspoon beef bouillon granules
1 pkg. (6 tablespoons) sauce mix
½ teaspoon salt
¼ teaspoon black pepper
Place all ingredients into a quart jar, placing milk, sauce mix, pepper, salt, and bouillon granules into a small zip baggie to be placed on top of potatoes in the jar. Place lid on jar & store in a cool dry place until ready to use. Decorate as desired. *Yield: 4 one-cup servings.*
Tag Instructions: To prepare, brown 1 pound of ground beef in a skillet, and drain off excess fat. Add 2 ¾ cups water to jar contents. Heat to boiling, reduce heat, cover and simmer stirring now and then, for about 25 minutes or until the potatoes are tender.

Raisin & Brown Sugar Instant Oatmeal

Pinch of salt
6 teaspoons brown sugar
6 tablespoons raisins
6 plastic sandwich bags
3 cups quick oats
1 ¾ teaspoons cinnamon
Put ½-cup oats in blender and blend at high speed until powdery. Reserve in a small bowl, then process another ½-cup oats. Into each bag, put ¼ cup unchopped oats, 2 tablespoon powdered oats, and a scant ¼-tsp. salt. Seal and store packets in an airtight container. Decorate if desired.
Tag Instructions: To make oatmeal, empty a packet in bowl and add ¾ cups boiling water. Stir and let stand 2 minutes. Enjoy!

Scalloped Potatoes

3 cups dehydrated potatoes
1 package (6 tablespoons.) sauce mix
1/3 cup nonfat dry milk
Put sauce mix and dry milk into an individual, small zip baggie with air removed. Place the potatoes into the bottom of a 1-quart jar, then add the baggie of mix/milk on top. Place lid on jar and store in a cool dry place until ready to use. Decorate as desired.
Tag Instructions: To prepare potatoes, add:

½ teaspoon dried oregano, crushed
½ cup small shell macaroni or other small pasta
¼ cup dry lentils
¼ cup dried chopped mushrooms (optional)
Mix all ingredients and layer in an airtight container. Store, tightly sealed, until needed. Decorate as desired.

Tag Instructions: To prepare, combine jar contents with 3 cups water in a 2-quart saucepan. Bring to boiling; reduce heat. Cover and simmer 40 minutes, or until lentils are tender, stirring occasionally. Remove from heat. Serve hot and enjoy! *Yield: 3 side dish servings.*

Rainbow Bean Soup

14 lbs. assorted dried peas, beans and lentils in the following 8 varieties for a layered, colorful appearance:

White beans
Split peas
Small red beans
Red lentils
Red kidney beans
Pinto beans
Pink beans
Lentils
Great northern beans
Black-eyed peas
Black beans
Baby lima beans
12 beef flavor bouillon cubes
12 bay leaves

Layer beans in jars. Add ¼ cup of each type of bean to the jars, layering the beans. Choose thc most colorful bean for the bottom layers of the jar. Add eight ¼ cup layers to each jar. Place 1 bay leaf and one bouillon cube on top of the beans in each jar. Seal each jar. Decorate as desired. *Yield: 12 gift jars.*

Tag Instructions: To prepare, rinse and sort beans in a large pot. Add 6-8 cups cold water. Let stand overnight, or at least 6 to 8 hours. Drain soak water and rinse beans. To cook, place beans in a large pot and add:

Bouillon cube
6 cups water
1 can (14 oz.) Chopped tomatoes in juice
1 bay leaf

Simmer gently until beans are tender, about 2 hours. Season to taste with salt and pepper.

Split Pea Soup

2½ cups pearl barley (16 ounces pkg.)
2½ cups lentils (16 ounces pkg.)
2½ cups green split peas (16 ounces pkg.)
2 cups alphabet macaroni (8 ounces pkg.)
1½ teaspoon white pepper
1½ teaspoon thyme
1 cup dried onion flakes
½ cup parsley flakes
½ cup celery flakes

Mix all ingredients together. Store in a jar with a tight-fitting lid. Stir before using. *Yield: 10 cups of mix.*

Tag Instructions: To prepare, combine 1 cup of soup mix with 4 cups of water or seasoned stock in large pan. Add 1 cup of cooked chopped meat, if desired. Bring to a boil. Reduce heat to low and cover pan. Simmer gently for 45 to 60 minutes, or until peas are tender. Add ½ teaspoon of salt if desired. Enjoy!

Stone Soup

2½ cups green split peas (16 ounce pkg.)
2½ cups lentils (16 ounce pkg.)
2½ cups pearl barley (16 ounce pkg.)
2 cups alphabet macaroni or brown rice
1 cup dried onion flakes (2 3/8-oz. pkgs.)
½ cup celery flakes (1 3/8-oz. pkg.)
½ cup parsley flakes (1 ¼-oz. pkg.)
1½ teaspoon thyme
1-½ teaspoon white pepper

Mix all ingredients together. Store in a jar with a tight- fitting lid. Stir before using. *Yield: 10 cups of soup mix.*

Tag Instructions: To prepare, combine 1 cup of soup mix with 4 cups of water or seasoned stock in large pan. Add 1 cups of cooked chopped meat, if desired. Bring to a boil. Reduce heat to low and cover pan. Simmer gently for 45 to 60 minutes, or until peas are tender. Add ½ teaspoon salt, if desired. Enjoy!

SEASONINGS/DRESSINGS/OTHER

Down Home Chicken Gravy

¾ cup instant flour
1 1/3 cups instant nonfat dry milk powder
3 tablespoon instant chicken bouillon granules
¼ teaspoon ground sage

⅛ teaspoon ground thyme
⅛ teaspoon ground pepper
½ cup butter or margarine
Layer the ingredients in the order given in Mason jar. Seal tightly, decorating jar if desired.
Tag Instructions: To prepare, combine milk powder, instant flour, bouillon granules, thyme, sage and pepper. Stir with a wire whisk to blend. Cut in butter or margarine until evenly distributed. Spoon into a 3-cup container with a tight-fitting lid. Label with date and contents; store in the refrigerator. Use within 4-6 weeks.

Enchilada Seasoning Mix
2 teaspoon minced onion
1 teaspoon salt
1 teaspoon paprika
1 teaspoon dried chili pepper
1 teaspoon corn meal
1 teaspoon chili powder
½ teaspoon sugar
½ teaspoon minced garlic
½ teaspoon ground cumin
¼ teaspoon dried oregano
Combine all ingredients in a small bowl and blend well. Spoon mixture onto a 6-inch square of aluminum foil and fold to make airtight. Label or tag as Enchilada Seasoning Mix. Store in a cool, dry place. Decorate if desired. Must be used within 6 months. *Yield: 1 package (about 2 tablespoons) of mix.*
Tag Instructions: To use, mix together with a little water and a squeeze of lime juice, and use desired amount (to taste) when making beef or chicken enchiladas.

French Salad Dressing
1 teaspoon dry mustard
1½ teaspoon salt
1½ teaspoon paprika
¼ cups sugar
⅛ teaspoon onion powder
Combine all ingredients in a small bowl; stir until well blended. Put mixture in a foil packet or 1-pint glass jar and label or tag as French Dressing Mix. Store in a cool, dry place and use within six months.
Tag Instructions: To make salad dressing, combine 1 packet of jar mix, ¾ cup vegetable oil, and ¼ cup vinegar in a glass jar. Shake until well blended. Chill before serving. *Yield: 1¼ cups of dressing.*

Italian Dressing
Pinch of pepper
2 tablespoon grated parmesan cheese
1½ teaspoon granulated sugar
1 teaspoon dried minced onion
1 tablespoon dried parsley leaves, crushed
½ teaspoon dried sweet basil leaves, crushed
½ teaspoon celery seed
¼ teaspoon ground thyme or marjoram
¼ teaspoon ground oregano
¼ teaspoon garlic powder
⅛ teaspoon salt

Combine all ingredients in a small bowl, stirring until evenly distributed. Wrap airtight in heavy-duty aluminum foil and label. Store in a cool, dry place. Decorate if desired. Use within six months. *Yield: 1 package (4 tablespoons)*

Tag Instructions: To make dressing, you will need:
1 package (4 tablespoons) Italian Dressing Mix
1/3 cup red wine vinegar
¾ cup vegetable oil

Place all ingredients into a pint jar and stir or shake until well blended. Cover and refrigerate 30 minutes before serving. *Yield: 1 cup of dressing.*

Moist Pie Crust Mix
5 lbs. (20 cups) all-purpose flour
3 lbs. can vegetable shortening
3 cups cold water
2 tablespoon salt
¼ cup all-purpose flour (if desired)

Combine flour and salt in a very large bowl. Mix well. With pastry blender cut in shortening until evenly distributed. Mixture will resemble cornmeal in texture. Add cold water all at once and mix lightly until the flour absorbs all the water and texture resembles putty. If dough is too sticky, sprinkle a little flour over the top and mix until dough barely holds together in the bowl. Divide dough into 10 oblong rolls. Wrap each roll well with plastic wrap and heavy foil. Freeze and label as Moist Pie Crust Mix. Use within 12 months. *Yield: 10 rolls of mix; enough for 20 single piecrusts.*

Tag Instructions: To prepare crust, partially thaw 1 roll of mix. Divide dough into two balls. Roll out dough to desired thickness between two sheets of lightly floured wax paper. Place dough in a 9-inch pie plate without stretching. Flute edges. If filling recipe calls for a baked piecrust, preheat oven to 425 degrees. Bake 10 to 15 minutes until very lightly browned. Cool. If your pie recipe calls for an unbaked crust, fill with desired ingredients and bake according to directions for filling.

Nana's Pie Crust Mix

5 cups vegetable shortening

2 tablespoon salt

12½ cups all-purpose flour

Combine flour and salt in a large bowl and blend well. With a pastry blender, cut in shortening until evenly distributed. Mixture will resemble cornmeal in texture. Put in a large airtight container and label as Flaky Pie Crust Mix. Store in a cool, dry place and use within 10 to 12 weeks. Or put about 2 ½ cups of mixture each into 6 freezer bags. Seal and label bags and freeze. Use within 12 months. *Yield: 16 cups mix, enough for 12 single piecrusts.*

Tag Instructions: To make a flaky pie crust, add:

2 ½ cups Flaky Pie Crust Mix

1 tablespoon white vinegar

1 large egg, beaten

¼ cup ice water

Crumble mix (if frozen). Place in a medium bowl. In a small bowl, combine ice water, egg and vinegar. Sprinkle one spoonful of the water mixture at a time over the flaky piecrust mix and toss with a fork until dough barely clings together in the bowl. Roll out dough to desired thickness between 2 sheets of lightly floured wax paper. Place dough in 9-inch pie plate without stretching. Flute edges. If your pie recipe calls for a baked piecrust, preheat oven to 425 degrees. Bake 10 to 15 minutes or until very lightly browned. Cool. If your recipe allows for an unbaked crust, simply fill per your filling preference (follow that recipe's instructions) and bake according to directions.

Pizza Crust Mix

2 teaspoon salt

2 ¾ cups bread flour

1 tablespoon active dry yeast

In a medium bowl, combine all the ingredients. Place the mix in an airtight container. Decorate if desired. *Yield: Dough for two 12-inch pizzas.*

Tag Instructions: To prepare pizza crust, you will also need:

2 tablespoon olive oil

1/3 cup freshly grated Parmesan

1 teaspoon crushed oregano

1 cup warm water

1 cup tomato sauce

½ cup grated mozzarella cheese

Place the Pizza Dough Mix in a large bowl & add the oil and water. Beat with a wooden spoon or dough hook until mixture forms a ball. Turn out onto a floured board and knead for 5 minutes. Transfer to a greased bowl and let the dough rise for 90 minutes. Divide the dough in half and pat into two 12-inch circles. <u>For thin crust</u>, fill and bake the pizzas now. <u>For thicker crust</u>, let pizzas rise 30 to 45 minutes. Top the pizza dough with tomato sauce, cheeses of your choice, crushed oregano, and olive oil drizzled over the pizzas. Add other toppings as you see fit (adjust baking time accordingly). Preheat the oven and bake at 425 degrees for 20 to 25 minutes or until done. Let stand 5 minutes. Enjoy!

Savory Beef Gravy Mix
3 teaspoon brown sauce for gravy
3 tablespoon instant beef bouillon granules
1 1/3 cups instant nonfat milk powder
¾ cup instant flour
½ cup butter or margarine
¼ teaspoon onion powder
⅛ teaspoon ground thyme
⅛ teaspoon ground sage

Tag Instructions: To prepare, combine milk powder, instant flour, bouillon granules, thyme, onion powder and sage. Stir with a wire whisk to blend. Cut in butter or margarine until evenly distributed. Drizzle brown sauce for gravy over mixture. Stir with wire whisk until blended. Spoon into a 3-cup container with a tight-fitting lid. Label with date and contents; store in the refrigerator. Use within 4-6 weeks.

Sloppy Joe Mix
1 teaspoon salt
1 teaspoon green pepper flakes
1 teaspoon cornstarch
1 tablespoon instant minced onion
½ teaspoon instant minced garlic
¼ teaspoon dry mustard
¼ teaspoon chili powder
¼ teaspoon celery seed

Combine all ingredients in a small bowl until well blended. Spoon mixture onto a 6-inch square of aluminum foil and fold to make airtight. Label or tag as Sloppy Joe Seasoning Mix and store in a cool, dry place. Decorate if desired. Must be used within 6 months. *Yield: 1 package (about 3 tablespoons) of mix.*

Tag Instructions: To prepare, brown 1 pound lean ground beef in a medium skillet over medium-high heat. Drain excess grease. Add seasoning mix, ½ cup water, 1 (8 ounce) can of tomato sauce and bring to a boil. Reduce heat and simmer 10 minutes, stirring occasionally. Serve on hamburger buns. Enjoy!

Taco Seasoning

2 teaspoon instant minced onion
1 teaspoon salt
1 teaspoon chili powder
½ teaspoon instant minced garlic
½ teaspoon ground cumin
½ teaspoon crushed dried red pepper
½ teaspoon cornstarch
¼ teaspoon dried oregano

Combine all ingredients in a small bowl and blend well. Spoon mixture onto a 6-inch square of aluminum foil and fold to make airtight. Label or tag as Taco Seasoning Mix. Store in a cool, dry place. Decorate if desired. Must be used within 6 months. *Yield: 1 package (about 2 tablespoons) of mix.*

Tag Instructions: To make tacos, brown 1 pound lean ground beef in a medium skillet over medium-high heat; drain the excess grease. Add ½-cup water and the seasoning mix. Reduce heat and simmer 10 minutes, stirring occasionally. Remove from heat. Fill taco shells of choice and add trimmings as desired. Enjoy! *Yield: filling for 8 to 10 tacos.*

BEVERAGES

Chai Tea

6 whole cloves
6 cardamom seeds
4 whole black peppercorns
4 rounded teaspoon loose black tea
3 tablespoon honey
1 bay leaf
1 8" cinnamon stick or ½ teaspoon ground cinnamon
½ teaspoon ground ginger
¼ teaspoon ground allspice

Mix together all dry ingredients and store in a tightly sealed jar. Decorate as desired.

Tag Instructions: To serve, mix jar contents in a medium saucepan with 6 cups of water and bring to a boil for 5 minutes. Add 2 cups of milk and bring to a gentle simmer (do not boil). Allow the mixture to simmer until it reaches the desired strength, up to an hour. Add honey and stir to dissolve. Strain tea and serve immediately. *Yield: 6 servings.*

Fruit & Spice Tea
2 teaspoons cinnamon
1 teaspoon nutmeg
1 packet unsweetened cherry Kool-Aid
1 cup unsweetened instant tea powder
1 cup granulated sugar
1 (15 ounce) jar orange breakfast drink (such as Tang)
½ cup sweetened lemonade
Mix together all ingredients well. Store in a tightly sealed jar. Decorate as desired.
Tag Instructions: To serve, stir 2 teaspoons to 2 tablespoons (depending on size of cup and your taste) of tea mix into hot or cold water.

Island Tea
1 (15 ounce) jar of instant orange breakfast drink mix
1 cup sugar
1 cup unsweetened instant tea powder
½ cup presweetened lemonade-flavored soft drink mix
1 teaspoon each: imitation pineapple extract and imitation coconut extract
In a blender or food processor, combine all ingredients. Store in a tightly sealed jar. Decorate as desired. *Yield: 4 ¼ cups of tea mix.*
Tag Instructions: To serve, stir a rounded tablespoonful of mix into 6 ounces of hot water. Enjoy!

Mulling Spices Mix (Gift W/Bottle of Wine or Jug of Cider)
6 whole nutmegs (1 ounce)
3 boxes (1 ounce each) cinnamon sticks
2 tablespoon finely chopped, crystallized ginger
1/3 cup chopped dried lemon peel
1/3 cup chopped dried orange peel
¼ cup whole cloves
¼ cup whole allspice
Place cinnamon sticks and nutmegs in a heavy plastic bag and crush with a rolling pin to create small pieces. Mix with remaining ingredients. Store in an airtight container and decorate as desired. *Yield: enough spices for 14 batches of mulled wine or cider.*
Tag Instructions: To mull wine, stir ½-cup water and 1/3 cup sugar in a 1 ½ to 2-quart pan over medium heat until sugar dissolves. Add a 750-ml bottle of wine (3 ¼ cups). Place three generous tablespoon of mulling spices in a tea ball or muslin or cheesecloth bag and add to pan. Reduce heat to low, cover and heat very gently until mixture is very hot but not boiling, about 20 minutes.

Discard spices. <u>To mull cider</u>, place 3 generous tablespoon of mulling spices in a tea ball or muslin or cheesecloth bag. Add to a half-gallon (8 cups) apple cider in a 2 ½ to 3-quart pan. Bring to a boil; reduce heat, cover, and simmer 30 to 35 minutes. Discard spices.

Russian Tea

2 cups orange breakfast drink powder (such as Tang)
1 teaspoon ground cinnamon
1 package unsweetened lemonade mix (enough for 2 quarts)
1 cup unsweetened, non-lemon flavored instant tea mix
1 cup sugar
½ teaspoon ground cloves

Mix together all ingredients well. Store tightly sealed. Decorate as desired.

Tag Instructions: To serve, stir 2 teaspoons to 2 tablespoons (depending on size of cup and your taste) of tea mix into hot water. Enjoy!

Thank you for your purchase!
May you enjoy and be well!

ABOUT THE AUTHOR

Rhonda Belle is a Tennessee native and a connoisseur of great tastes. Her culinary delights are inspired by her Southern roots. She sums it up this way:

I am from cornbread and cabbage, fried chicken and Kool-Aid soaked lemon slices.

I am from hen houses, persimmon trees and juicy, red tomatoes on the vine.

I am from sunflowers growing wild in summer and homemade ice cream in the winter.

I am from family reunions, blue collar men, happy housewives, and Sunday dinners.

I am from spiritual folks who didn't always get it right, but believed in the power of prayer – and taught it to their kids.

I am from the hottest of hot summers and kids running barefoot and free through thirsty Tennessee grass.

I am from a grandmother who sang gospel that was magic…song drenched air would tumble from her lungs, leap into your spirit and make you feel fantastic things.

I am from hard, heartfelt lessons about living and kitchens full of the perfume of love.

♥♥♥ This book is from my heart to yours. ♥♥♥

For Freebies and New Book Announcements:

Follow @SoDelishDish on Twitter!

And Rhonda Belle (SoDelishDish) on Facebook!

Made in the USA
Middletown, DE
03 August 2022

70471252R00022